YOUR KNOWLEDGE HAS VALUE

- We will publish your bachelor's and master's thesis, essays and papers

- Your own eBook and book - sold worldwide in all relevant shops

- Earn money with each sale

Upload your text at www.GRIN.com
and publish for free

Bibliographic information published by the German National Library:

The German National Library lists this publication in the National Bibliography; detailed bibliographic data are available on the Internet at http://dnb.dnb.de .

This book is copyright material and must not be copied, reproduced, transferred, distributed, leased, licensed or publicly performed or used in any way except as specifically permitted in writing by the publishers, as allowed under the terms and conditions under which it was purchased or as strictly permitted by applicable copyright law. Any unauthorized distribution or use of this text may be a direct infringement of the author s and publisher s rights and those responsible may be liable in law accordingly.

Imprint:

Copyright © 2017 GRIN Verlag
Print and binding: Books on Demand GmbH, Norderstedt Germany
ISBN: 9783668691520

This book at GRIN:

https://www.grin.com/document/421552

Kat Szydlowska

The Success of Wikipedia. Models and Concepts

GRIN Verlag

GRIN - Your knowledge has value

Since its foundation in 1998, GRIN has specialized in publishing academic texts by students, college teachers and other academics as e-book and printed book. The website www.grin.com is an ideal platform for presenting term papers, final papers, scientific essays, dissertations and specialist books.

Visit us on the internet:

http://www.grin.com/

http://www.facebook.com/grincom

http://www.twitter.com/grin_com

Table of Contents:

Table of contents………………………………………………………………...2

1. Introduction……………………………………………………………….....3

2. Resource Based View Model……………………………………………..4

2.1 VRIN………………………………………………………………….........4

2.2 SWOT………………………………………………………………………..5

3. Blue Ocean Strategy ……………………………………………………..9

3.1 Differentiation and low cost……………………………………………….9

3.2 Four-action strategy framework…..……………………………………….10

3.3 The three strategy propositions…………………………………………..12

4. Chaos Theory……………………………………………………………...13

5. Conclusion………………………………………………………………...14

References………………………………………………………………….15

1. Introduction

It is not possible nowadays to imagine the Internet without Wikipedia, which is the prime online information source for millions of people. It is undoubtedly one of the most popular websites in the world and accommodates a crucial number of readers and contributors. Beutler (2014) compares the Wikipedia to "the passion project of a volunteer community committed to developing a universal knowledge base". Wikipedia has grown to be the sixth most popular website worldwide behind websites such as Google or Yahoo! (500 Global Sites Index, 2013). The infrastructure of Wikipedia enabled the contributors to build the largest and most up to date encyclopaedia in the world. Wilson &Likens (2015) pinpoint the accuracy of the website, which is similar to the traditional reference sources like for instance Encyclopaedia Britannica.

By using different models and concepts, this paper tries to find out the feasible reasons for its ultimate success. Based on the Harvard Business Review Case Study on Wikipedia, the Resource- Based View model is utilized, where the strategic capabilities of the Wikipedia are analysed. Also, this paper argues how Blue Ocean strategy can provide a sound explanation of the apparent strategic success of the most popular online encyclopaedia.

2. Resource- Based View Model

The Resource- Based View model (RBV) postulates that resources are valuable, rare, inimitable and non-substitutable (VRIN) and can build a platform upon which firms may accomplish a competitive advantage (Brown, 2013; Callaway& Jagani, 2015). Resource-based view fundamentally tends to highlight that a possession of strategically useful, heterogeneous, and not replicated by competitors' resources constitutes the resource position of the firm among rivalry companies (Apostolakis et al, 2012). Simon et al, (2012) gives example of Mercedes Benz car group as a company where strategic capabilities such as innovation, technical knowledge and quality of service were utilized to gain a competitive advantage.

2.1 VRIN

Value

The greatest value provided by Wikipedia is its availability to anyone without any charge. The advantage is that Wikipedia is a free encyclopaedia and can be freely read without getting permission from any other party, therefore the users are able to access it anytime and share with others without any constrains. Wikipedia is being led by the main innovators and leaders hence it has become a global movement to free knowledge.

Rarity

The technology, which Wikipedia uses in protecting the integrity of its articles is rare and unique, therefore if any inappropriate changes are implemented into Wikipedia's articles, they are normally repaired within very short period of time. This is possible thanks to automatic tracking mechanisms, which exhibit any modification made by registered users, thus the integrity of the articles is preserved.

Inimitability

Wikipedia is most likely to be chosen as the main source of news and reference information when one carries out a keyword search on the well known engines today such as Google or Yahoo. It is very probable to find Wikipedia at the top of the list of recommended pages, which it is unlikely to happen as far as its competitors are concerned. Wikipedia aligns value, profit and people propositions around both differentiation and low cost, therefore this gives Wikipedia significant competitive advantage over other online encyclopaedias in the market.

Non-substitutability

There is a potential possibility of being replaced by another substitute, however what is not to be replaced is the esteem which is associated with the brand name, therefore Wikipedia is able to acquire new customers while at the same time retaining the old ones.

2.2 SWOT

In order to achieve a full usefulness of the Resource- Based View (RBV) approach, an individual ought to consider it as representing the strengths and weaknesses of a company. In additional way, the external environment could possibly play the space to form opportunities and threats for the organisation. In this regard, an informal environment of a SWOT analysis could possibly be formed (Nham and Hoang, 2011).

A SWOT (strengths and weaknesses, opportunities and threats) analysis can "serve as a catalyst to facilitate and guide the creation of marketing strategies that will produce desired results" (Santos & Laczniak, 2015). In the view of Addams & Alfred (2013), SWOT is extremely valuable and inevitable for decision making in estimating a company's environment in fast changing, competitive and thoroughly diversified world. Although this framework can be criticised for instance for oversimplify more complex business situations (Strategic Direction, 2015), it is recommended for the organisations to utilizing SWOT to assess their wellness and establish the steps to improve operations in the future.

Strengths

Wikipedia is a free online encyclopaedia, while in order to have full access to the articles of its competitors Britannica and Encarta, an individual is obligated to pay for it. Hence, this led to exit of Encarta as an online encyclopaedia and decrease in popularity of Britannica.

Wikipedia is one of the most popular online search engines today, therefore when someone performs a keyword search; it is most likely that the Wikipedia will be the website which will turn up.

The articles on the Wikipedia are available in over 270 different languages including smaller languages such as Maori or Upper Sorbian; hence many people from all over the world are able to read the articles in their own language, whereas the competitors offer information only in English. Thus, this gives Wikipedia a significant competitive advantage over its competitors.

Wikipedia has a strong sense of community among its virtual citizens. An extensive kindness campaigns are carried out in order to acknowledge the exceptional effort, skills and commitment shown by their particular contribution.

Wikipedia's administrative overheads are very low thanks to team of dedicated volunteers. Thus, the online encyclopaedia is able to offer a great value to its customers.

Weaknesses

Wikipedia is a non-profit website, which is run by significant number of volunteers, however very few of them have the experience and knowledge of a professional writer or editor, therefore this can lead to many mistakes and errors on the site.

One of the most crucial issues for Wikipedia is vandalism, which the site is likely to be susceptible to. Vandalism is easy to commit on Wikipedia, because anyone is able to edit the content of the website. For instance, on May 26, 2005, it was falsely written that John Seigenthaler- a retired journalist was a suspect in the assassination of both Kennedy and his brother, US President John F. Kennedy. This act of vandalism stayed for 132 days on the website before it was removed.

In contrast with traditional encyclopaedias, Wikipedia is not formally reviewed by the experts, thus any medical or scientific article might be written by an amateur and will not be reviewed or edited by any medical professional or scientist.

Wikipedia's articles can vary in terms of quality, factuality or trustworthiness, therefore it is not recommended to use Wikipedia as the only source for a research purposes. As a matter of fact, most educational institutions do not regard the online encyclopaedia as a genuine, citable source at all.

Furthermore, because of the fact that the Wikipedia's articles can be at different stages of editing, they are unusable and are not of encyclopaedic quality from the start.

The most popular online encyclopaedia has very large number of its contributors. They come from different background and their opinions differ from each other. Various editors form the content of each article therefore in the end a state of neutrality can be accomplished where no one's point of view is reflected. However, this process can take a very long time.

Threats

Since Wikipedia launched in 2001, the numerous websites have emerged which can constitute a potential threat to the future of the website. The most popular competitors are: the Scholarpedia, Encyclopedia for Life or Encyclopedia.com. Similarly to Wikipedia, these websites are free of charge, yet what distinguish them from the most popular online encyclopaedia is the fact that articles have been approved by an actual scholars, thus its is much better free resource for research papers for students rather than Wikipedia.

Another problem comes from finding and keeping its contributors. The number of people writing and editing entries is shrinking. Hence, this can lead to a serious threat to the future of the organisation.

The below figure 2.2 shows the number of editors for the English-language version has decreased by a third in seven years:

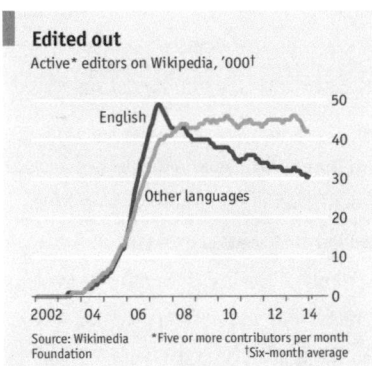

Figure 2.2. Active editors on Wikipedia
Source: The Economist (2014)

One of the most significant threats for the future of Wikipedia are change- resistant and innovation- averse communities who are "stuck in 2006 whereas the rest of the users in Internet are thinking about 2020 and the next three billion users" (Lih, 2015). Thus, the tensions might appear among the long-time editors, new editors or foundation employees which are very hard to resolve.

Opportunities

Wikipedia seeks to entirely embrace mobile as a medium for reading and editing, therefore the Wikipedians will be able to contribute through their mobile devices. This trend has been already observed in Korea, where 25% of its editors have contributed using their mobiles.

Wikipedia's aim is to reach every language on Earth. At the moment the articles on the websites are available in 270 languages, but there are still many more to go.

Another opportunity lies in reaching by Wikimedia's Foundation multiple cultural institutions such as government, libraries or museums that can provide the website with a new material.

Wikipedia's goal is to expand in terms of adding significant amount of multimedia to its content, thus the tools ought to be form which enable for collaborative creation and editing of audio and video.

3. Blue Ocean Strategy

Blue Ocean Strategy was created by Chan and Maubourgne of INSEAD University in France (Becker, 2013). Kim and Mauborgne (2015) classified the organisations into either Red Ocean or the Blue Ocean. According to the authors, in attempt to beat the competitors, rivalry becomes extremely intense, where water turns bloody thus red ocean annotation. The space grows crowded and the growth possibilities significantly decrease (Alhaddi, 2014). In contrast, the Blue Ocean constitutes "all the industries not in existence today" where markets are not established to certain extent, industry boundaries are not determined, therefore there is very weak or no competition. In Blue Ocean, high growth rates can be anticipated (Emiel et al, 2012). Kim and Mauborhne (2015) give the example of Cirque du Soleil as an organisation following Blue Ocean Strategy, which combines opera and ballet with the circus, which established a completely new kind of live entertainment (Shaker, 2016).

3.1 Differentiation and low cost

Blue Ocean Strategy is based on the simultaneous pursuit of differentiation and low cost. It tends to break the value-cost trade-off, therefore reducing and eliminating factors, which are competitive within an industry as well as creating and raising factors the industry has never offered (Randall, 2015).

Wikipedia distinguishes itself from the competitors, because it provides a range of various and applicable articles in diverse languages and makes a continuous effort in updating these articles to enhance their readability, clarity and accuracy. The website now offers articles in over 270 different languages mainly in English, German or French; therefore majority of people internationally can easily access the website in their own language. Furthermore, what differentiates Wikipedia from its competitors is that it is often being placed in the top five of the most popular online search engines behind websites such as Google or Yahoo.

Wikipedia follows both differentiation and low cost at the same time. Full access to all its articles is available to anyone with Internet access without any charge. It provides premium value, while keeping its administrative overhead very low. This is possible thanks to dedicated team of numerous dedicated volunteers. Unlike its competitors, Wikipedia's writers, editors or even board of trustees are all volunteers; therefore there is no cost involved.

3.2 Four-action strategy framework

Blue ocean strategy creates a blue ocean of uncontested market space by providing systematic frameworks and tools in order to separate from the competition, therefore in presenting this strategy for retaining existing customers and attracting non-customers, Kim and Mauborgne (2015) utilised a four action framework, which they referred to as the 'eliminate-reduce-raise-create grid'(ERRC) as shown in Figure 3.2 below:

Eliminate	Reduce
Those factors or elements that no longer have value or may even detract from value for customers.	Those attributes that have been over-designed in the race of competition, or those have little attraction of customers.
Raise	Create
Those attributes that can result in significant value for customers, or those that have high attraction to customers.	Those factors that can discover new sources of value for customers or those that can create new demand and attract noncustomers.

Figure 3.2: Four action framework
Source: Yang & Yang (2011)

Eliminate
Wikipedia completely eliminated the cost associated with accessing the articles. While only a portion of the articles on Britannica.com and Encarta.com are available for free, one would have to pay an annual subscription of $70 and $30respectively for a premier membership. However, Wikipedia's articles do not charge its users neither in form of fees or any advertisements; hence they can enjoy a free access to the website unlike its competitors.

Create
Wikipedia's aim was to create a free encyclopaedia, where everyone could gain an easy access to the information without getting permission from anyone. In order to enable the users of the online encyclopaedia utilize, copy and update its articles, Wikipedia introduced joint licenses therefore it developed a win-win situation by abolishing the restrictions globally in order to constantly increase the human knowledge and discover latest

applications for the product, whereas the intellectual integrity and financial interests of the original authors are being protected.

Reduce

Wikipedia significantly reduced its costs associated with the paying its employees since Wikipedia's writers, editors and even boards of trustees are volunteers, therefore significant cost could be saved. By contrast, the biggest competitor- Britannica maintains a paid editorial board of large number of advisors, contributors or editors.

Raise

The Wikipedia managed to receive multiply contributions from individuals all over the world, for example they raised $8.1 in 2009-2010 fund drive which is almost double $4.4 million raised in 2007-2009. Hence the organisation was able to build up its technical capacity to offer even more knowledge projects around the world.

3.3 Three Strategy Propositions

Blue ocean strategy presents how to combine the three strategy propositions - value, profit, and people. The aim is to make sure the company is allied around the new strategy and that it generates a win for buyers, the organisation, and for stakeholders and employees.

In order for the strategy to become successful and feasible any company ought to create offering which buyers are attracted to. It has to develop a business model which allows an organisation to create substantial profit and hast to provide the employees with the motivation in order for them to implement successfully the strategy.

In Wikipedia three propositions are aligned, therefore the buyers, an organisation as well as internal and external stakeholders benefit to great extent.

Value Proposition

Value is the critical factor why people decide to utilize Wikipedia as an online source of information. Unlike the biggest competitor Britannica, it is free of charge and articles can be read by anyone who has internet access.

Profit Proposition

The most popular online encyclopaedia generated a substantial profit proposition hence this allowed its parent company, the Wikimedia Foundation to collect new funds so that administrative and marketing costs could be lowered. As a result, new funds are applied to make the website more accessible and expand the base of its contributors.

People Proposition

People in Wikipedia consist of the entire staff, corporate partners and large number of dedicated volunteers all over the world, who are extremely committed to supporting vision and mission of the organisation. Thanks to them, the administrative overhead can be kept at low level. It is very important that employees and business partners are committed in implementing a strategy otherwise this can lead to an execution failure.

4. Chaos Theory

Chaos theory was initially pioneered by Lorenz's work on the dynamics of turbulent flow in fluids. He developed his interest in chaos in 1961 by accident while working on weather prediction. Yet, for the past fifty years chaos theory found interest in various fields such as mathematics, computer science, politics or economics (Guo et al, 2009). Chaos theory believes that a wide set of phenomena are not predictable and it is impossible to anticipate the future: It concentrates on events which are not predictable, follow unknown rules, have no logical consequence and tend to challenge rational description. Briefly, it is not unlike decisions made under conditions of extreme uncertainty. Hence, the chaos theory establishes the position of bounded rationality for instance that human information-processing abilities are restricted (Mina, 2012).

The chaos theory gives an insight into Wikipedia's explosive growth. Wikipedia was found in 2001, the year where the world of Internet was still relatively new to many people worldwide. Its first endorsement was gained from the Slashdot website and later in the year, the website found new contributors who were willing to write the articles. The biggest breakthrough for Wikipedia which contributed to its explosive growth, was its collaboration with Google. The website directed thousands of new visitors to Wikipedia, thus spreading the word of its place on the Internet. According to "The Estate Gazette" (2015), collaboration is vital for the survival of the business. This means getting rid of an organisational mindset, which was based on hierarchies, seniority, process and order. It is essential nowadays, since the world has moved from the organisational to the networked era. The world is changing rapidly, it is driven by technological advance and what has worked in the past, will fail to work in the future. The old framework and structure which managed the way we live and the organisations fail to cope with the speed of the change.

Another important factor, which significantly contributed to explosive growth of Wikipedia and created the "chaos" is world of mouth. For example, although Microsoft tried hard to make his own version of digital encyclopaedia, it did not succeed straight away. However, the word of mouth allowed Wikipedia to become a common household name. The users of this website feel valued; therefore they become very committed to the brand. Nowadays, Wikipedia established its position as the greatest reference websites, with presently 400 million unique visitors every month and more than 90,000 active contributors (Xin & Xiaoquan 2013).

5. Conclusion

Wikipedia is one of the most popular website in the world in most countries with unrestricted access to the Internet. Its success is associated with the fact that it accomplished the high profile by effectively deploying its resources. This paper which is based on the Harvard Business Review Case Study on Wikipedia used the Resource- Based View Model- VRIN and SWOT which analysed the organisation's strategic capabilities. Furthermore, it has been discussed by utilizing conventional strategic management models and frameworks such as ERRC to what extent the Blue Ocean strategy provides a sound explanation of strategic success in Wikipedia.

The paper also tried to gain an insight into online encyclopaedia's explosive growth by looking at the chaos theory.

It has been proved that what gives the Wikipedia the competitive advantage over other online encyclopaedias in the market, is the fact that it was able to align value, profit and people propositions around both differentiation and low cost. Yet, what needs to be taken into consideration is the fact that in order for the Wikipedia to stay so successful, it needs to constantly evolve and innovate since the millions users of Internet already are thinking about the next technological progress which can take place within next few years.

References:

Beutler, W., 2014. Wikipedia's future hinges on adapting its structure. PRweek, 17(2), pp. 23.

Top 500 Global Sites index Alexa [Internet]. 15 Dec 2013. Available: Alexa.com/topsites. Accessed 15 December 2013

Wilson, A, & Likens, G 2015, 'Content Volatility of Scientific Topics in Wikipedia: A Cautionary Tale', Plos ONE, 10, 8, pp. 1-5, Academic Search Premier, EBSCOhost, viewed 13 April 2016.

Brown, R.S., 2013. Capabilities, strategic intent and firm performance: An empirical investigation, Temple University.

Callaway, S.K., PHD. and Jagani, S.B., PHD., 2015. Strategic Context for Internet Banking: How Traditional Banks Manage e-Commerce to Build IT Capabilities and Improve Performance. Journal of Internet Banking and Commerce, 20(1), pp. 0_1, 1-21.

Apostolakis, C., Rodriguez, J.C. and Gomez, M., 2012. A Resource-Based View Model in Achieving Entrepreneurial Innovation for Canadian Universities, 09 2012, Academic Conferences International Limited, pp. 17-XII.

Simon, A., Kumar, V., Schoeman, P., Moffat P. and Power, D., 2011. Strategic capabilities and their relationship to organisational success and its measures.Management Decision, 49(8), pp. 1305-1326.

Nham, P.T. and Hoang, V.H. (2011) "Building an integrated framework of strategic management theories to explain performance of firm in one industry", Journal of Global Management Research

Santos, N, & Laczniak, G 2015, 'Marketing to the poor: A SWOT analysis of the Market Construction Model for engaging impoverished market segments', Social Business, vol. 5, no. 2, pp. 95-111. Available from: 10.1362/204440815X14373846978589. [11 April 2016]

Addams L. and Allfred A.T., 2013. "The first step in proactively managing students' careers: teaching self-SWOT analysis". Academy of Educational Leadership Journal, 17(4), pp. 43-51.

Is SWOT analysis still fit for purpose? 2015. *Strategic Direction,* 31(4), pp. 13-15.

The Economist, 2014, "The future of Wikipedia" online source, available from: http://www.economist.com/news/international/21597959-popular-online-encyclopedia-must-work-out-what-next-wikipeaks [8 April 2016]

Lih,A, 2015 "Can Wikipedia Survive?" online source, available from: http://www.nytimes.com/2015/06/21/opinion/can-wikipedia-survive.html [9April 2016]
Becker, H., 2013. Imax Move To Hollywood: Blue Ocean Strategy or a case of who moved my cheese, 2013, Institute for Business & Finance Research, pp. 472-476.

Kim, W.C. & Mauborgne, R. (2015) „Blue Ocean Strategy: How to Create Uncontested Market Space and make the competition irrelevant", Harvard Business School Publishing Corporation, Expanded Edition, USA

Emiel F.M. Wubben, Dusseldorf, S. and BATTERINK, M.H., 2012. Finding uncontested markets for European fruit and vegetables through applying the Blue Ocean Strategy. *British Food Journal,* 114(2), pp. 248-271.

Shaker, 2016, 'Making change your way', PM Network, 30, 1, p. 23, Business Source Premier, EBSCOhost, viewed 25 March 2016.

Randall, R.M., 2015. W. Chan Kim and Renée Mauborgne dispel blue ocean myths. Strategy & Leadership, 43(2), pp. 11.

Yang, C, & Yang, K 2011, 'An integrated model of value creation based on the refined Kano's model and the blue ocean strategy', Total Quality Management & Business Excellence, 22, 9, pp. 925-940, Business Source Premier, EBSCOhost, viewed 25 March 2016

Guo, X, Vogel, D, Zhou, Z, Zhang, X, & Chen, H 2009, 'Chaos Theory as a Lens for Interpreting Blogging', Journal Of Management Information Systems, 26, 1, pp. 101-127, Business Source Premier, EBSCOhost, viewed 11 April 2016.

Mina S., 2012. Managing the strategic decision in governmental organization within chaos theory, Babes Bolyai University, pp. 28-33

Chaos Theory. 2015. The Estates Gazette, pp. 32-33.

Xin Xu, S, & Xiaoquan (Michael), Z 2013, 'Impact of Wikipedia on market information environment: evidence on management disclosure and investor reaction', pp. 1043-A10, Business Source Complete, EBSCOhost, viewed 14 April 2016.

YOUR KNOWLEDGE HAS VALUE

- We will publish your bachelor's and master's thesis, essays and papers

- Your own eBook and book -
  sold worldwide in all relevant shops

- Earn money with each sale

Upload your text at www.GRIN.com
and publish for free